# Vortex of Our Affections

*poems by*

# Claire Ibarra

*Finishing Line Press*
Georgetown, Kentucky

# Vortex of Our Affections

Copyright © 2017 by Claire Ibarra
ISBN 978-1-63534-300-7 First Edition
All rights reserved under International and Pan-American Copyright Conventions.
No part of this book may be reproduced in any manner whatsoever without written permission from the publisher, except in the case of brief quotations embodied in critical articles and reviews.

## ACKNOWLEDGMENTS

"A Formulaic Love Story" appeared in *Words Dance*, Issue 14, 2013 and *Eye to the Telescope:* "Science" issue, 2014. (print and online)
"The Astronomer's Wife" appeared in the *"Point Mass" Poetry Anthology* by Kind of a Hurricane Press in 2013. (print)
"Big Fish" and "Things the Prose Poem Says" appeared together in *White Stag*, Ars Poetica Issue, 2015. (print)
"Flame Tree" and "Yin-Yang in the Sky" and "Weight of Silence" appeared together in *Praire Wolf Press Review*, Issue X, Fall 2016. (online)
"Ambien" appeared in *Van Gogh's Ear* in 2014. (online)
"Bang, Bang" appeared in *Literary Orphans*, Issue 22, 2015. (online)
"In the Space Between" appeared in *Blue Fifth Review,* October 2012. (online)
"The Gringa Can Dance" appeared in *Flash Frontier*, "Dance" Issue, 2016. (online)
"Silk Threads" appeared in Vol. 7, Issue 15 of Pirene's Fountain, 2014. (print)
"Reunion" appeared in *Lummox 2,* "Place" Issue, 2013. (print)
"Thirst" appeared in the July 2012 edition of *Thrush Poetry Journal*. (online)
"Slitting the Cushions" appeared in *San Francisco Peace and Hope*, Vol. 5, 2016. (online)

Publisher: Leah Maines

Editor: Christen Kincaid

Cover Art: Photograph by Claire Ibarra
Credit: NASA, ESA and the Hubble Heritage Team (STScI/AURA)-ESA/Hubble Collaboration

Author Photo: Nan Altman

Cover Design: Elizabeth Maines McCleavy

Printed in the USA on acid-free paper.
Order online: www.finishinglinepress.com
　　　　also available on amazon.com

Author inquiries and mail orders:
Finishing Line Press
P. O. Box 1626
Georgetown, Kentucky 40324
U. S. A.

# Table of Contents

A Formulaic Love Story ................................................................. 1

The Astronomer's Wife ................................................................. 4

Big Fish ............................................................................................ 5

Yin-Yang in the Sky ....................................................................... 6

Rinse and Recycle .......................................................................... 7

Ambien ............................................................................................ 8

Bang, Bang ...................................................................................... 9

In the Space Between .................................................................. 10

The Gringa Can Dance ............................................................... 11

Silk Threads .................................................................................. 12

Flame Tree .................................................................................... 14

Reunion ......................................................................................... 15

Thirst ............................................................................................. 16

Belonging ...................................................................................... 17

Love Is ........................................................................................... 18

U-Haul Mausoleum .................................................................... 19

Weight of Silence ......................................................................... 20

Heading West ............................................................................... 21

Slitting the Cushions .................................................................. 23

Ars Poetica: Things the Prose Poem Says ............................... 24

## A Formulaic Love Story

[H$_2$O]

She is a lovely mermaid; he is Poseidon. They are still young.
Salt water heals wounds, so they bathe together during low tide for hours on end.

[AgBr]

They are sensitive to all things of consequence. Images become
clearer in their dreams, only to fade into phantoms, like the shroud of Turin.
They can't remember the details, of all they meant to say.

[Al$_2$CoO$_4$]

She dreams of living inside a Maxfield Parrish, with gold-rimmed clouds, luminous skies of iridescent blue—the color of Chinese porcelain, of tinted glass.
It's the color that makes her happiest.

[AIO]

Exploding grenades. He was trained to deny love. You can't kill another human being while believing in it. Now he lives with PTSD. She gives him renewed hope, nurses his spirit with the droplets of a slow and gradual baptism, a baptism of an ancient love.

[N$_2$]

If it is not solid, if it doesn't fit into the palm of her hand, it will float out of the atmosphere and disappear into empty space.
That has always been her fear.

[CH$_3$COCH$_3$]

She keeps her nails long, and they click against cups and scratch his flesh, giving him shivers. She wears blue polish. She uses yellow rubber gloves to wash the dishes.

[FeO]

He can't write without a delete button. Permanence never suited him. The Earth's crust is tattooed with etchings, the stories of loss and extinction. Her stories will become etched in sunspots and wrinkles—his in a receding hairline.

[B(OH)$_3$]

The cruelty of sprinkling acid on fire ants nags at her—and yet she knows they can be deadly. She marvels that something that can cure athlete's foot also slows the rate of fission. She believes their love is a lot like that.

[CH$_3$CH$_2$OH]

Alcohol is the oldest recreation known to man, even Neolithic people drank spirits. Residue was found on 9,000 year-old pottery in China. How can she argue with that?
Scientific evidence supports his cause.

[CH$_2$O]

They cling to each other after death visits. Though his drinking gets in the way. But how can she deny him those sips of comfort, those sips of redemption, those sips of forgetting pain.

[O$_3$]

They are protected from ultraviolet rays. The atmosphere is inviting, as he watches her belly grow. They bask in the Florida sun and their extended family becomes tolerable. They discuss moving to Kansas.

$[I_2]$

The sea is rich, and so they continue their bathing ritual at low tide, and she buys iodized salt. Most anything can be purchased fortified.

$[As_2O_3]$

In the highest altitudes of the Alps, live the "arsenic eaters of Styria" who believe the poison gives them strength. Arsenic is homeopathic. There's a risk to cures, there's a risk in loving someone too much.

$[Fe_3O_4]$

When they first met, he had a moustache, a beard, and
abundant dark chest hair. She loved to twirl it around her fingers.
He was a man, she felt like a little girl.

$[H_2]$

He tells her that he wants to jump out of a plane on his 50th birthday.
Parachuting, parasailing, hot air balloons. Air travel will get him nowhere.
She knows what he wants is elusive.

$[Au(OH)_3]$

Their wedding bands are inscribed with the date of their anniversary, lest they forget that day. Forget the years joining like molecules, into formulas of strange and magnificent creations.

### The Astronomer's Wife

Our Nebulae of love
Forms clouds and dust
With photons of color
He kisses my belly
I am his star factory
Within a vacuum of space
Forms a heavenly pocket

Our child will be born to
Reconcile dark matter
We are born, live, and die
As dwarfs and giants
Growing in clusters
Thousands of light years
Merely arc seconds

**Big Fish**

She cooks dinner. She is wearing a white apron with red apples on it. She fries eggs, boils hand grenades, sautés her children. Then the refrigerator opens its door and swallows her in one gulp—just like how the big fish swallowed Jonah.

She lives in the cold cavern. She builds a fire to keep warm, but vegetables, like damp kindling, fill the cavern with black, heavy smoke. She likes it in there, it isn't like the outside, where everyone tries to feed her and make her fat. Inside, she is alone and hidden in smoke, and she converses with skinny asparagus and pink, fleshy salmon. The salmon tells her, "You can leave anytime you wish." She replies, "I think not." Green worms crawl out of the red apples on her apron, they smile and wiggle. The worms grow tiny little arms, and tiny little legs, and big, round, soft heads. She places them in her mouth and swallows, so they can live safe inside her belly—just like how the big fish swallowed Jonah. Or maybe how the old lady swallowed a fly.

**Yin-Yang in the Sky**

It's the super blood-moon lunar eclipse and the penumbra creates
a giant Yin-Yang suspended in the sky, mimicking the balance
between light and dark—and the forces of our obstinate love.

Darkness slowly eats the light, the sliver grows ever smaller.
I hear neighbors yell and cheer the touchdown on TV,
like Mayans cheering astronomical predictions unfolding.

Children play on the street, while parents watch the celestial show,
and this makes me love humanity: the willingness to face our ancient gods.
A plane flies in front of the night's battle, light quivers, darkness takes over.

The golden halo around the edge of the blood-red moon shines like my
wedding band, showing me that our love is bigger than the sky,
even bigger than my imagination. The moon stays dark for so long,
I begin to worry about rotation.

Then the neighbors and children become quiet. Planes cease their flights
across the sky.
I imagine life on another planet, in another galaxy, and what it means—
strange gravity, new constellations, swirling nebulae.

I feel the emptiness and distance of that other world, until the neighbor
shouts, "Oh shit," at the football game. Bringing me back to this Earth,
to the eternal battles between light and dark, and to our stubborn Yin-Yang
love.

**Rinse and Recycle**

Passion unrestrained,
anger teetering with
sentimental love.
Indiscriminate random taste,
binges without preference.
She poured the left over
booze and pills down
the kitchen sink,
rinsed the empty bottles.
Dragging the bin to the curb,
to be picked up by morning,
dry leaves and dirt
clung to her slippers.
She learned the word
enabler. So it began:
Al-Anon, books with
co-dependent in the title,
New Horizons—
a mental health clinic.
There the carpets were
stained and pastel
landscapes hung
crooked on the wall.
They sat in a circle,
hashing it out, until
their lives were purged
and scrubbed and
sanitized—yet in the
end left degraded.

**Ambien**

If you had a car, you would drive to 7-Eleven and eat burritos with a construction worker named José. Instead you take another pill and drink a bottle of wine. Slip, sliding away to Paul Simon. Shave your head, just the sideburns. Then you let your wife find the razor and the empty bottle and the pink elephants dancing in tutus around the room singing, "After Midnight" to Clapton's electric guitar. Light white candles and pray "Hail Mary" on your knees, slip sliding away and cursing your wife for an imagined infidelity. Face paint, hair clogging the bathroom sink, paella dumped on the kitchen floor, a cut that needs stitches, long distance calls, ants marching through cracks in the walls. Your wife calls the doctor to send for help, you dream that they haul you off to the loony bin.

Here you find peace, here you find redemption, here you find God. Here you see your father who died, your brother who died, your sister who died, and they speak to you in tongues and you understand the meaning. Here is where you are, here is where you are lost, here is where you disconnect from your physical self and become an empty self, who no one understands, as if you're speaking in tongues, the language of death, the language of a very deep sleep.

## Bang, Bang

Bang!
Bang, bullet to the temple
Temple walls crumble
Crumble the body
Body of decay
Decay of muscles, tissues, joints
Joints bulge and swell
Swell and erode like a river
River rushes and pounds
Pounds on a hollow drum
Drum of a landside
Landside devours the inside
Inside is birth.

Birth, don't cry—fight—pull the trigger
Trigger empty space of quiet
Quiet the voices of disdain
Disdain the negative
Negative void—black hole—of space
Space of a two-dimensional hologram
Hologram of the universe that scientists now say only reflects a third dimension and theories prove it's true
True to thy self
Self-delusion is safe
Safe as any drug
Drug the impulse
Impulse ignited the Big Bang.
Bang!

**In the Space Between**

There is nothing but empty space between us,
He says one night in the darkness
I marvel because I know it's true
I had read a Quantum Physics book, and from it
Understood that the ground, the walls are not solid
Nothing is solid at all

Diminutive solar systems: atoms
Orbiting sun-like nuclei mirror our vast galaxy
Bodies too, are mostly empty space
But where he sees nothingness,
I see symmetry, two universes coexisting
Both constructed out of dying stars

When he leaves, there is only the
Indentation of his body in the bed
In that space, I still feel reverence and love

**The Gringa Can Dance**

People say we married too young. But when we danced it was all hands on hips and gentle sways to Mambo Kings and *Besame* that would turn into rhythmic steps and stomps to the congas of Tito Puente. You'd take my hand to make me twirl. Your hands didn't need to touch my body, as I mimicked your deft feet, followed your moves to Celia Cruz. You would sweat while I purred. We vowed to name our firstborn after the *Queen of Salsa*, and we did.

The *gringa* can dance, they'd say. But I knew it was just a matter of finding your groove, not thinking too hard, losing myself to your allure and pull. It was all electric and fiery heat, and so who could blame this *gringa* fool. My feet burned inside those high-heeled shoes.

The nights ended in Tango: firm embrace, slow gliding steps and low dips, where I would lose my footing and ground. But your arms held me up, until they didn't. And the collapse was complete and no holds barred. Maybe our marriage wouldn't last, but baby, we sure could dance.

**Silk Threads**

The front gate is locked,
purple bougainvillea dried and withered—
faded, fragile, thin
    as moth wings.

Fruit trees: ripe chirimoyas, limes,
avocados had dropped to the earth in
abundance. Now the trees are dusty and barren.

When a grandmother dies, a mother dies,
and a small corner of the world is buried—
a world of silk threads
    woven into shawls,
        ponchos, scarves.

Worms in wooden plank beds, feast on
mulberry leaves, weave cocoons, emerge into
dull moths, who lay their eggs and promptly die.

Children live on, marry, have children,
become widowed—leaving a
husband's guitar in the corner
    without strings
        to gather dust.

Recalling music of brighter days,
they will remember the song and dance,
roosters chasing hens, the scent of
cinnamon and roses, the spinning of raw silk
    into thread.

Now the dog lives alone,
behind the locked gate, emaciated
and lonely, longing for his housemother,
who had cared for these living things
    until she became ancient
        —blind, deaf, crippled.

The life cycle of silkworms leaves less tattered
    a garment.

**Flame Tree**

During long walks in balmy June, I try to capture the vivid, fiery blossoms of the Poinciana. My lens tames the Flamboyant tree.

Even with filters and enhancements, the scarlet-orange corollas dim, compared to their brilliance set against sunlight and slate blue sky.

I stand beneath the royal branches, looking up at loaded boughs bending with the weight of crimson clusters—inflorescence among feathery leaves.

Looking down, the sight of crushed vermillion petals pressed into black asphalt reminds me of childhood road trips and bugs smashed against the windshield.

The blossoms of India—peacock flowers also bring back images of the vibrant, narrow streets of Katmandu.

During the Dashain Festival, I stood enthralled by flowers, incense, and altars for the blessings of telephones, cars, bicycles, and televisions—all matters of earthly possessions.

On the eighth day, the goddess Kali, the Dark Mother, is appeased by sacrifices. I looked into the eyes of a decapitated goat, as a man rushed by holding the head by its ear.

The shouts of the crowds, putrid smells and grime and human defecation around temple walls clouded and faded the beauty of those flowers.

Now, empty pods, left as skeletons after birthing seeds, rest among the fallen petals at my feet. The flame of color—refusing to be stored in my camera...

**Reunion**

My mother offers me a cup of tea,
red zinger swirls, turning
steamy water a vibrant pink.

It took me ten years to find her.
In the silence between us, wind chimes
clang like we're in a cathedral.

I drum my fingers on the Formica table,
a dream catcher hangs from the ceiling fan,
my eyes follow its circular motion.

She scoots to the kitchenette, places the
kettle back on the hot plate. I look out a
a tiny window at the empty landscape.

Her trailer sits at the edge of Death Valley.

She tells me it's her sanctuary, soothing
sand dunes, cactus blooming twice a year.
Jack rabbits come around by day, coyotes
howl at night, one bit the tip of her dog's tail.

My mother musters the will to tell her stories,
of tea with Jesus on a space ship,
her lover, Irene, the one she left with,
about Uncle Ray and his slithering ways.

When it's time for me to leave, she grabs the
King James from an easy chair. The dog is
at my side, wagging his stubby tail.

The setting sun turns the sand dunes golden,
the sky a shade of purple. I watch my step to the car,
coyotes get mean when searching for a meal.

**Thirst**

On a dirt road in Death Valley
I encountered a lone coyote
We contemplated one another

Hungry from meager sand dune fare
We looked to the distant peaks
Of the mercurial Amargosa Range

In Shoshone land is Hell's Gate
Where one can balance on Dante's Ridge
And salt beds glisten like petrified snow

Alluvial fans are skeletons of waterways
One year back in 1929, there was
No rainfall at all, not a drop

I asked the coyote, do you rain dance?

## Belonging

While self-medicating, you might think you've encountered Angels and feel you belong to them, more than you belong to this World. You might spend entire your life searching for that connection: in lovers, in the cracked teacup, in the broken vase, in the white grout stained black with mold.

Why are Gurus so happy? They are fat but not heavy. Their soft bellies—round like the full moon—obscure lotus-crossed legs. You can't open your hips so wide. When asked if Aliens have visited our planet, they smile and laugh and laugh. Wood-beaded rosaries shake and dance to the rhythm of chuckles and chants.

You completed the Holy Sacraments before becoming a Secular Humanist. The plain wafer, the sweet wine, rewards after the torment of your first Confession. That was before you realized, with Sea Level Rise, we will all be Baptized—one way or another.

**Love Is**

Bukowski said, "Love is a dog from hell." And now I better understand you—

You must be the reincarnate of some belligerent, drunken poet who mocks my fragile, fissured marriage.

Your stinky, black fur, sticky from the sweat of your fury.
Nips to bites, Prozac masking anxiety, unsettled nerves.

Once a shy, sweet puppy, you developed a macho swagger,
jumping walls, chasing street cats, and I think, what an asshole.

I offered you shelter, from the homeless shelter,
where you sat on the cold tile floor behind glass.
Now your guard dog instincts are haywire
because you hate to see my suitcases packed.

When you rest your head on the hard floor, like a drunk in
an empty tub, stumpy tail beating against the white wall,
you give me that look, you know the one, doleful eyes
with Buddha-like knowing—

Love and suffering: wet and dry food served in the same bowl.
And I can't help but think—

You might be a dog from hell, but you're my little demon,
all mine, my little Bukowski.

**U-Haul Mausoleum**

They filled the 10x15 cement room with boxes and bedframes, stacked limbs and bones of a dead marriage.

It was better than the alternative, which might have involved weaponry— A blowtorch to belongings, bulldozing and butchering.

They blindly constructed scaffolding with mattresses, picture frames, dining room chairs—to be scaled like the Tower of Babel.

The windowless room was suffocating, forced labor under an electric blanket, the packing and unloading their sacraments and sacrifice.

Out of this burial would be water birth, while years of collecting, years of marriage, rot away in the heat and mildew of a storage grave.

**Weight of Silence**

Presence in the weight of silence:
piano keys longing for scales in C,
hummingbird wings deadened in snow,
the burn and itch of a fresh tattoo.

Resist nostalgia—the lure of
whitewashed memories splashed
over crumbling graffiti walls.

Instead, slip under the heavy quilt,
listen for Beethoven in the hollow belly,
smell the scent of hibiscus in spring,
Vaseline the ink of that painful burn—

of your loss.

# Heading West

1.

Sometimes Life turns feral. Sometimes it snarls and hisses in your face. I woke from a deep sleep to find mine had gnawed and clawed through the door, it jumped the fence, taking a backwoods trail, leaving only faint tracks behind. Perhaps it seeks refuge from the winter storm.

I look to the constellations,
to the rising and setting sun,
to the lopsided curve of the waxing moon,
to the tilt of the rotating Earth.

I look to my compass and map,
and now head west to find it.

2.

There was something about the way you said goodbye. It left me thinking about trekking the Himalayas, about reaching basecamp and finding it littered with the remains of expeditions. Trash strewn over the mountainside—leftovers of heroic feats.

We trekked the Inca trail, you leading the way, stumbling and swerving, me following behind dreaming my fumbling dreams. Looking back, we never walked side by side.

There was silence in the end. No shouts, nor cries of rage. Just scrambled eggs and buttered toast, you sipped strong, black coffee like a cowboy on the range. I drank mine with sugar and cream.

Time to leave turquoise waters, palm tree shadows, hurricane season and perpetual summer.

I made plans for the road trip, packing the car, my list of essentials: playlists for every mood, camera for small town attractions like diners and dinosaur bones, audio book of the latest bestseller, a jug of water, bag of dried fruit.

As I head out, I wonder, would the west be any kinder to my fumbling dreams?

3.

Skim wetlands, bogs and sinkholes,
cold-blooded creatures sunning on asphalt.

Paul Simon sings Graceland, as I
trampoline through streets of lost dreams.

Black asphalt singes my tender, bare feet
dancing in the streets of New Orleans.

The Rockies roll me in bare tundra, laced
with rivers of wild flowers ablaze with color.

I'm heading west, where hippies dance
and deserts are set ablaze with Burning Man
and cactus flowers—
     night blooming, vibrant, rare.

I'll swim in the Eel River, while
Jerry Garcia plucks his acoustic guitar
back from the Dead—
     singing sweet, rare, vibrant.

I fly in lucid dreams over junkyards,
brushing my palms over scraps of metal
     diamonds of broken glass.

California holds me in her palm, me, the
girl with long curls, so kinky people stare.

Rough diamonds scatter, east to west,
     skimming my redwood blanket of dreams.

**Slitting the Cushions**

Lying in this soft bed,
in this soft suburb, in this soft city,
I want to punch through it, to find
the jagged edges and sharp points
to jab myself awake.

Today were more attacks.
Weapons of choice: assault rifles, explosives, Twitter.
I wanted to feel outrage and grief.
But I asked, what will I do with the rest of my life?

I wonder how many of us lie in our soft beds,
encased in a soft suburb, silently jabbing
our wounds and scars?

I use thin blades to slit smothering
soft tissue and membranes of memory,
so that this world is not cushioned by
my disbelief.

# Ars Poetica: Things the Prose Poem Says

*Inspired by Boxing Inside the Box:*
*Women's Prose Poetry by Holly Iglesias*

    I can put everything the prose poem says into a list. This comforts me. Lists transform chaos into order. Lists make the unruly more manageable. Lists make me feel in control, even when I'm not. The prose poem is a quadrilateral. It loves boxes and squares. It tells me that my vagina is in the shape of a box, not round and smooth like an ovoid or sphere. Love has sharp edges and dark, hidden corners. It also tells me that my orgasms are a she, and that this she has her own feelings, and thoughts, and wants to be independent from me. But what if my orgasms were a he? That would complicate things considerably. The best place to listen to the prose poem is in front of my bathroom mirror. Not only is the mirror a perfect rectangle, but it also reflects my image. Here I can become meditative and go very deep, beyond the surface of things, and think about my childhood, and my marriage, and my own children. What is the shape of childhood? What is the shape of my marriage? I ask. It tells me the shape is crooked, and bent, and full, like a very old woman. The old woman has a belly like an overripe fruit, but the rest of her is made of twigs. The prose poem says it will only tell me the truth, so if I don't want the truth then I shouldn't even bother to ask.

Claire received her MFA in Creative Writing from Florida International University. Her poetry, fiction, and creative nonfiction have appeared in numerous anthologies and literary journals. Her poetry has appeared in such fine publications as *Pirene's Fountain, Thrush Poetry Journal, Midwest Quarterly,* and *"America Is Not the World"* by Pankhearst Publishing. Claire enjoys photography as a means of storytelling, as well. Claire has worked with nonprofits, teaching creative writing to incarcerated women in Florida. Currently, she teaches and lives in Denver, Colorado.

www.ingramcontent.com/pod-product-compliance
Lightning Source LLC
LaVergne TN
LVHW041523070426
835507LV00012B/1772